Starlight and Candleglow

Best wishes,

Helen Louise Marshall

1971

Also by Helen Lowrie Marshall

Bright Horizons
Close to the Heart
Dare to Be Happy
Aim for a Star
Hold to Your Dream
The Gift of Wonder
Walk the World Proudly
Quiet Power

HELEN LOWRIE MARSHALL

Starlight and Candleglow

ILLUSTRATED BY PAUL BACON

1971

DOUBLEDAY & COMPANY, INC.

GARDEN CITY, NEW YORK

Designed by Joseph P. Ascherl

Library of Congress Catalog Card Number 74-147254
Copyright © 1971 by Helen Lowrie Marshall

Dedicated to
families everywhere

CONTENTS

STARLIGHT AND CANDLEGLOW

Starlight and candleglow –
    And hearts are led each year
    Into the warmth and fellowship
    Of Christmas love and cheer.

Starlight and candleglow –
    And memory's bright embers
    Stir the thoughts to happy hours
    The Christmas heart remembers.

Starlight and candleglow –
    And eyes are given to see
    The place of peace and brotherhood
    This world was meant to be.

Starlight and candleglow –
    And every shining ray
    Leads mankind one step nearer
    The Christ of Christmas Day.

– – And hearts are led each year
Into the warmth and fellowship
Of Christmas love and cheer.

THE SOUNDS OF CHRISTMAS

These are the sounds of Christmas
    That mean so much to me –
The sounds that say "It's Christmas!"
    In my growing family.

The lisping baby voice that struggles
    Through a Christmas rhyme,
The grade-school band in carols played
    A bit off tune and time.

The giggling in the closets,
    And the whispering on the stair;
The secrets that just *will* pop out
    In spite of all their care.

The blessed temporary peace
    From little quarrels and taunts;
The carefully veiled questioning
    To find what each one wants.

The rattle of the piggy banks
    With Christmas savings stored;
The grave decisions as they spend
    Their tiny precious hoard.

The shrieks of sheer exuberance
    That greet the Christmas tree;
The "Jingle Bells" and "Silent Night"
    So heartily off key.

The fire crackling on the hearth,
    The popcorn's bursting cheer,
The happy noise of girls and boys
    In parties gathered here.

These are the sounds of Christmas
    That mean the world to me –
The sounds of love within the heart
    Of my own family.

CHRISTMAS INVENTORY

We have a Christmas card list
In a book thumb-worn with age,
And every year we painfully
Go through it, page by page.

We both agree it simply
Isn't sensible at all
To keep on sending cards to folks
We barely can recall.

And so we settle firmly down,
Determined to strike out
The names of everyone that we
Have any doubts about.

"Now, here are two," I'll say,
"We never see them any more."
Then John will say, "Well, no,
But isn't that what cards are for?"

"It lets them know we're still alive
And hope that they're the same."
And so we vote to keep them,
And go on to the next name.

"Now, who the deuce is this?" John says,
"Here's one we needn't send."
"Oh, no!" I wail, "We can't drop her –
She once was my best friend."

And so it goes, page after page,
And when we're finally done,
We find the list is still intact –
We haven't dropped a one.

In fact, it's even longer
Than it ever was before.
There always are a few new friends
To swell the mounting score.

Just how it all will end
If this continues, Heaven knows –
But still, you know, it's kind of nice
To have a list that grows.

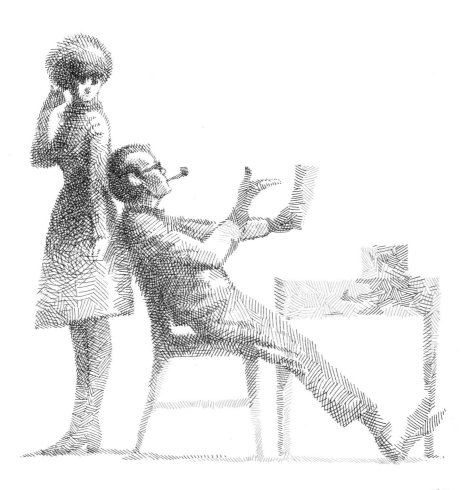

THE CHRISTMAS PICTURE

"Time for the Christmas picture!"
    Father booms above the noise
Of the little and the middle
    And the grown-up girls and boys.

"All right, folks, how about it?
    Uncle Martin, Cousin Sue –
Grandpa, Grandma – Where's the baby?
    Gotta have him in it, too.

"Come along, kids, leave your toys there,
    This will only take a minute.
This year we want a picture
    That has everybody in it.

"Move in closer, all you youngsters;
    Scrooch down just a little, Ed,
If I get the kids there on the floor,
    I can't quite get your head.

"That's better – now I got you.
    Now – say cheese when I count three –
On second thought, though, maybe
    We should group around the tree.

"Let's try it. There, Aunt Ellie –
    Grandma, you sit in the chair;
The rest of you stand natural-like,
    It doesn't matter where.

"A little closer, though – and Ed,
    Scrooch down a little more.
Why don't you kids try standing up,
    And Ed sit on the floor?

"There, that's better – I'm afraid, though,
    That it's not good composition;
Too much detail – let's all move back
    Into our first position.

"What's the matter with the baby?
　　Oh, you had to wake him up.
Quiet, everybody! Junior,
　　Do you have to hold the pup?

"There now, that's a better background –
　　Just that one big wreath of holly.
Now – a big smile, everybody –
　　'Tis the season to be jolly!

"Hold real still and watch the birdie,
　　Try and not look at the light.
One – two – three – Ding blast it!
　　That's the third bad bulb tonight!

BAFFLED BOXER

Wrapping Christmas packages
　　Is great fun, I'll admit,
But it would help sometimes
　　If one could find a box to fit.

Now, I have stacks of boxes –
　　I can't throw a box away –
My empty-box collection
　　Is a pure joy to survey.

And why there never is a box
　　To fit the need at hand,
Is one of those enigmas
　　I shall never understand.

But I shall keep on saving them.
　　Discouraged? Not at all.
Sometime there simply has to be
　　A box that's not too small.

HEY, MOM – GUESS WHAT!

I'm gonna be a Wise Man!
I'm in the Christmas Play!
I gotta thing to carry
An' some words I gotta say.

I hafta wear a bathrobe,
An' I getta wear a beard!
John Henry can't be in it
'Cause he gets too skeered.

I'm wearin' Jimmy's bathrobe,
'Cause it covers up my pants;
An' I gotta take a bottle
For my frenkincanse.

I'm gonna wear a yellow towel
Wrapped up around my head.
The Wise Guys used to dress that way –
That's what our teacher said.

You see, a coupla other guys and me
Walk down the aisle,
An' nen we all three put our gifs
Together in a pile.

An' nen we get down on our knees
Right on a special spot,
An' nen I got some words to say,
But I forget now what.

It's gonna be a real swell play –
You *gotta* come and see!
Jes' watch for Jimmy's bathrobe,
An' the guy in it is me!

SURROUNDED BY LOVE

Ma spends days fixin' up the house
    For Christmas time each year,
With mistletoe a-hangin' down
    From every chandelier.

Candles on the window sills
    And, naturally, a tree –
We even hang our stockings up,
    Though there's just her and me.

But then the cards begin to come
    And Ma will sigh, "Oh, dear,
I plumb forgot to fix a place
    For Christmas cards this year."

We start by settin' them around
    Among the plants and pictures,
And hang a few around about
    On the electric fixtures.

We set 'em on the mantel piece
    And on each window sill.
You know, it's just amazin' how much
    Space them blame cards fill.

By Christmas, all Ma's decorations,
    And Ma, too, and me,
Are practically buried
    In a Christmas greeting sea!

And Ma says, "Land a-goshen,
    Ain't this living room a sight!
Next year I've got to fix a place
    To show the cards off right."

But, deep inside, we kind of like
    Cards scattered everywhere –
We sort of feel surrounded
    By the thoughts of those who care.

CHRISTMAS EVE–AND ADAM

"Christmas is really for kids," he said,
Then hustled the children off to bed.
Christmas only for kids, indeed!
You should have heard me scold and plead.
I might have known it was all in vain.
He *had* to run the electric train,
He had to try out Johnny's drums,
Junior's horn, the top that hums.
(How they could sleep through all that noise!)
Yes, Christmas is for little boys,
But age is not the measuring stick
Used by jolly old Saint Nick.
A man's a man all year – and then,
Come Christmas, he's a boy again.

THE LITTLEST CHERUB

He was the littlest cherub,
His wings – one low, one high –
His tipsy tinsel halo
All but covering one eye.

His hands, devoutly folded,
Were on the grubby side.
His shoes, so new and shiny,
Had one string come untied.

And he wiggled as he knelt there
Beside the bed of straw,
While friends looked on indulgently,
And smiled at what they saw.

The pageant went off smoothly,
It was lovely – so they said,
But I had eyes for only one –
That small, cropped haloed head.

My heart was filled to bursting
And my eyes were wells of joy,
As I thanked the Christ of Christmas
For this gift of one small boy.

THE TWENTY-FOURTH DAY OF DECEMBER

It's Christmas Eve by the morning sun,
    I note with a drowsy eye.
One more day and the frenzied time
    Till Christmas will have passed by.
I've a hundred and one last-minute chores,
    But before my toes touch the floor,
With a burst of noise four girls and boys
    Come tumbling through the door.

Their spirits high as the winter sky,
    They chatter like small magpies.
With Christmas so near, their holiday cheer
    Has nearly reached bursting size.
Then –"Jesus was borned in a manger."
    Our youngest, most pious one,
Injects a strangely gentling note
    Into the morning's fun.

"Borned in a barn of a manger
    Where the cows and the sheepses was,
And nobody knowed 'cept the shepherds.
    Do you want to know why-becuz?"
"Sure – Why-becuz?" the older three
    Chime in to get her started.
Pious she is, but our littlest, too,
    Is story-teller-hearted.

"'Cause nobody telled them, that's why," she shrugs,
    Mischief agleam in her eye,
"But the angels, they telled the shepherds.
    They was flyin' all over the sky.
And there was some Wisemen knowed it, too,
    This many – one – two – three –
And they was nice and brought some toys
    For Jesus's Christmas tree!"

Wherever the story may go from there
    Is anybody's guess,
So we shoo the lot of them out of the room
    And scamper them off to dress.
It's the twenty-fourth of December,
    And a busy day lies ahead,
But the worry is gone as I hum a song
    Smiling at what she said.

"Jesus was borned in a manger."
    I wonder if He grew to be
As impishly sweet as our own chatterbox
    When He was a starry-eyed three.
And my heart says a prayer as I run down the stair.
    Do you want to know why-becuz?
'Cause it's Christmas Eve and I firmly believe
    My family's the best ever was!

-- And memory's bright embers
Stir the thoughts to happy hours
The Christmas heart remembers.

SONGS OF CHRISTMAS

What is there about Christmas songs
    That makes us love them so?
This year – last year – the year before –
    A hundred years ago –

Then, as now, hearts thrilled to hear
    The grand old carols ring,
As happy carolers proclaimed
    The birthday of the King.

Now, as then, the magic of
    Each old familiar strain
Brings to mind the beauty
    Of the season once again.

We see the "little town of Bethlehem"
    In quiet lie,
Asleep beneath the glory
    Of that star high in the sky.

We sense the calm and peaceful hush –
    The gentle, radiant light
That brought "joy to the world" upon
    That "silent, holy night."

And when the children sing
    Of Santa Claus and jingle bells,
What glorious hope and happiness
    Their jolly music tells.

What is there about Christmas songs
    That makes us love them all?
Perhaps it's partly all the lovely
    Things that they recall.

TRADITION TIME

So much of the joy of Christmas
    Is the sameness of it all –
Always the wreath upon the door,
    The festoons in the hall;
The mistletoe hung overhead,
    The squeals at getting captured;
The sparkling tree that holds its viewers
    Silently enraptured.

The same beloved ornaments,
    The candles and the bells;
The same old Christmas stories
    That Grandpa always tells.
The same old battered angel
    Once again adds to the joy –
It's stood atop the tree each year
    Since Grandpa was a boy.

The merry family gatherings –
    The old, the very young;
The strangely lovely way they
    Harmonize in carols sung.
For Christmas is tradition time –
    Traditions that recall
The precious memories down the years,
    The sameness of them all.

FAMILY TREE

What a lovely tradition it used to be –
Grandmother's house for the family tree!
Uncles and aunties and cousins and brothers,
Sisters and babies and fathers and mothers –
The tree in the parlor, the gifts for each one –
Christmas at Grandma's – what glorious fun!

Turkey and cranberries, cookies and cakes,
Blissful ignoring of sure tummy-aches –
Noise and confusion and fun everywhere,
The house complete bedlam, but we didn't care.
Everyone beamed with a heartful of cheer
On Christmas at Grandma's house year after year.

A lovely tradition, but fallen in grace,
Now that I'm Grandma and our house the place
Where all the clan comes for the big celebration.
(Did we used to wreak such complete devastation!)
I ask in all humbleness, Grandmother mine,
However you managed a mien so benign!

I didn't appreciate all you went through
Until I became a Grandmother, too.
But after the noise and confusion all fade –
(I reckon it's just the way Grandmas are made) –
I find myself happily planning to be
Hostess next year for our family tree.

DO YOU REMEMBER?

Do you remember Christmas Eve
    The way it used to be,
When everybody gathered
    For the big church Christmas tree?

Remember crunching through the snow,
    The stars so very near,
A waiting stillness all about
    That you could almost hear.

And then the church, pine-sweet and warm,
    And all the friends you knew.
The program by the Sunday school,
    The "piece" you stammered through.

The boys, stiff in their Sunday best,
    And all the little girls
So happily self-conscious with
    Their unaccustomed curls.

The jolly padded Santa
    And the long-awaited minute
When you received that little bag
    With nuts and candy in it.

The happy sigh that lingered
    On the strains of "Silent Night";
The friendly Christmas wishes,
    So warm, so real, so right.

The last reluctant leaving
    Of the candlelighted tree –
Do you remember Christmas Eve
    The way it used to be?

CHRISTMAS BONUS

Oh, for those Christmas mornings
    With their good old-fashioned ways –
The thrill of waking with the dawn
    Upon that day of days!

The tree that had appeared
    As if by magic in the night;
The sheer, spine-tingling ecstasy
    Of gazing at the sight.

The stockings on the chimney place,
    The big orange in the toe;
The sound of sleigh bells echoing
    Across blue-shadowed snow.

The homemade gifts – the mittens
    We always knew we'd get.
We couldn't wait to get outside
    And get them wringing wet!

The good smells from the kitchen
    Meant a feast was on its way.
The turkey had less stuffing
    Than we kids on Christmas Day!

The uncles, aunts and cousins
    All descending in a whirl;
The shrieks beneath the mistletoe
    As Dad kissed every girl.

The carols round the organ –
    Mother pumping with a will.
Each year when I hear carols,
    It's those voices I hear still.

The Christmas times of Yesterday,
    What memories they hold –
A very special bonus for this
    Thing of growing old.

MEMORY TIME

Christmas Time is memory time –
    What memories we see
Reflected in the glow
    Of candlelight and Christmas tree.

Every Christmas stocking hanging
    From the mantel shelf,
Holds a happy memory
    Of that child that was ourself.

Each beloved carol brings back
    Voices now long still,
And memory's bright halo crowns
    Each candle on the sill.

Christmas time is memory time.
    In, oh, so many ways
Its happy sights and sounds recall
    The joys of other days.

– – And eyes are given to see
The place of peace and brotherhood
This world was meant to be.

WHAT IS CHRISTMAS?

What is Christmas? Wreaths of holly,
    Santa Clauses, fat and jolly;
Christmas trees and manger scenes,
    Jingle bells and evergreens;
Stockings on the fireplace,
    Happy smiles on every face;
Extra postmen on the beat;
    Special goodies; tired feet!
Stacks of mail, and crowded stores,
    Infinite last-minute chores;
Carol singing, candlelight,
    Christmas cards still left to write.

Sheer light-hearted happiness –
    All of this is Christmas – yes,
But it holds a deeper worth,
    This day of the Christ Child's birth.
In its mystic, magic way
    It continues to hold sway
Over men's hearts everywhere,
    Kindling their will to share.
What is Christmas? Love divine
    Moving through your heart and mine,
Bringing hope and love and cheer
    To the world year after year.

THE WONDER OF CHRISTMAS

This is the wonder of Christmas –
That it brings with each passing year
A rebirth of love and of friendship,
The spirit of good will and cheer.

That it purges away the harshness,
The callousness, hate and lust,
And hearts are transformed by its magic
To hearts full of faith, hope and trust.

This is the wonder of Christmas –
That its beauty never grows dim,
And over the centuries souls are led
By the light of the Star to Him.

WHICH ROAD?

Which road do we follow from Bethlehem?
    What is the way we take?
What is the course we should follow now
    At this New Year's daybreak?

Back to the same old way of life?
    Oh, but it's not the same –
For we have listened to angel song
    And have seen a star aflame.

And we have knelt by a manger bed
    And gazed with the Mother mild
On the living meaning of peace and love
    In the face of a sleeping Child.

What road do we take from Bethlehem?
    No road is too steep or far
If the road we take is for His dear sake
    And lit by His guiding Star.

CHRISTMAS EVE SERVICE

I saw the Christmas star shine out tonight
As brightly as upon that first midnight,
Its beam reflected from the Christmas skies
Aglow in warming depths of loved ones' eyes.

I heard the angels' song ring out as clear
As ever fell upon the shepherds' ear –
Angel voices borrowed from above,
As children's hearts poured out their song of love.

And oh, I saw the Christ Child, this I know,
As truly as the Wise Men long ago.
In every glowing candlelighted face,
I saw Him come and softly take His place.

CANDLELIGHTS OF MIRACLES

How many little miracles
    We witness day by day,
Miracles so commonplace
    We scarcely look their way.

A little act of kindness,
    A smile, a word of praise –
And no one knows how many lives
    Are changed – how many ways.

God's candlelights of miracles
    Kept lit by you and me –
Without their small far-reaching beams,
    How dark this world would be.

SOMETHING ABOUT CHRISTMAS

There's something about Christmas
    That brings out the best in us.
In spite of all the rushing
    And the hubbub and the fuss,
Deep down within our hearts we sense
    A peace that's oh, so right,
As we join in the chorus of
    The strains of "Silent Night."

There's something about Christmas
    That makes us want to be
The kind of person we'd be proud
    To have our neighbors see.
It clears away the shabby thoughts
    We've gathered through the year,
Replacing them with shining wreaths
    Of love and hope and cheer.

Remembering that little Fellow
    Born so long ago,
Somehow, makes even hardened hearts
    More soft and tender grow.
There's something about Christmas
    That rekindles faith grown dim
And strikes a note of peace and joy
    As we remember Him.

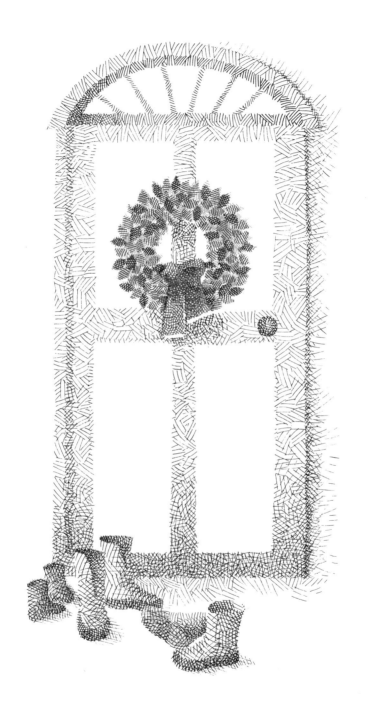

THE MIRACLE OF CHRISTMAS

Christmas is a miracle –
How else can one explain
The awesome power
Of the Christ Child's birth;
How through the ages it has crept
Into the hearts of men
And brought to light
Their finest, noblest worth?

How else can one account for
The feeling in the air
Of peace and warmth
And fellowship and cheer;
The hope it brings to saddened hearts,
The eagerness to share –
The triumph of the soul
This time of year?

It has to be a miracle –
No power but Divine
Could sweep the earth
With such a radiant light –
A miracle of love wrought deep
Within your heart and mine
In memory of the Christ
Of Christmas Night.

A LITTLE AT A TIME

We really should take Christmas
    A little at a time,
Stretching out its spirit through the year,
Giving little daily gifts
    Of love and thoughtfulness –
Widening its scope of special cheer.

We really ought to make it last
    Beyond the one short day,
And lend its candleglow to days between;
To spend our Christmas savings
    Here and there along the way,
And keep our Christmas spirit ever green.

We really shouldn't try to crowd
    Our feeling of good will
Into one day, no matter how sublime.
This world would be a better world
    If Christmas were spread out
And kept all year, a little at a time.

A SPRIG OF BRIGHTNESS

As we come away from Christmas
    To our old routine again,
Let us work a little harder
    Toward good will among all men.

Let us strengthen our resolve to use
    A little more restraint,
A little more compassion, and
    A little less complaint.

A deeper understanding
    And a great deal more of giving;
A bit more concentration
    On the finer side of living.

As we take down the Christmas tree
    And store the wreath away,
Let's keep a sprig of brightness
    To remind us of this day.

One little sprig of brightness
    To help us to remember
That love and cheer are not confined
    To one day in December.

ONCE-A-YEAR OUTBURST

Christmas begins in the heart of us all,
A deep-centered, Heaven-born part of us all,
A volcanic mixture of good will and cheer,
Erupting to overflow once every year.
How wide the spread of its happiness goes,
How deep and fruitful its joy, no one knows,
But some say that every good thing on this earth,
All noble causes and all things of worth
Are rooted in love that has spread from the flow
Of this yearly outburst of cheer we all know.

– – And every shining ray
Leads mankind one step nearer
The Christ of Christmas Day.

IN GENTLENESS AND IN BEAUTY

In the still of a winter's midnight,
    Christmas had its start,
In the soft, seeking cry of a Baby Boy
    Held to His mother's heart.

In the misty blue of a star's light
    Christmas came to earth,
With the echo of angel voices
    Singing the Christ Child's birth.

In gentleness and in beauty
    This Christmas time we share
Came to perform its miracle
    On men's hearts everywhere.

And still in the thoughtful quiet,
    In the midst of its merry joy,
The heart finds the meaning of Christmas
    In the gift of that Baby Boy.

THE RADIANCE OF LOVE

A Child was born in Bethlehem,
    Long, many years ago,
Wrapped in the radiance of love –
    A light whose afterglow
Lives on and on – and never shall
    Its gentle splendor cease
Till all the whole wide world shall know
    Its beauty and its peace.

MARY SPEAKS

No room in the inn?
There, Joseph, my dear,
Don't fret so. I'm sure
There must be some place near
Where we can find shelter
And rest for the night.
Have you noticed the stars –
How they seem overbright?
Such a beautiful sky!
Yes, Joseph, I heard –
"No room," the man told you –
I heard every word.
But he said he was sorry,
And meant it, I'm sure;
And he couldn't help it,
That man at the door.

But wait, there, he calls you.
Go, Joseph, and see –
Perhaps he has good news;
See what it can be....
The stable, you say?
Why, that will be fine!
You see, Joseph dear,
The bright stars were a sign!...
There, help me down, Joseph –
Your poor, tired feet!
How nice now to rest
On the straw, fresh and sweet.
And look, dear, the animals,
Peering to see

What sort of companions
These strangers can be!
And there in the sky,
Through that crack in the door –
That star – I've not seen

Such a bright star before.
How lovely it is,
And how good God has been.
How kind and how thoughtful
That man at the inn.
So much to be thankful for,
Dear, you and I,
A warm place to sleep,
A bright star in the sky –
I've never been happier –
Never before –
I pray God will bless him,
That man at the door.

ONE HUSHED MOMENT

For one hushed moment we see them there,
The three Wise Men with their treasures rare,
The lowly shepherds come to adore
The King they had so long waited for.
For one hushed moment – then lost to sight
In the deepening dark of Time's long night;
But for that moment each in his way
Lives in the heart of man today.

For one hushed moment of Time each year
Your heart and mine are given to hear
The angel chorus and see the star
Bidding us, too, come travel afar;
Bidding us come out of Doubt's dark night
Into the stable's holy light;
Bidding us follow the star's bright beams
Into the joy of remembered dreams.

For one hushed moment we sense the glory
The shepherds knew in the Christmas story,
And see, as the Wise Men saw above,
The radiant light of Peace and Love.
For one hushed moment in Time's swift race,
We pause in wonder before His Grace,
And life is richer and love more fair
For that hushed moment that we spend there.

CHRISTMAS WISH

There was brilliance, there was glory
When the angels sang that night;
There was wonder, awesome wonder,
In that fearful, lovely sight.

But inside the lowly stable
There was splendor shining, too,
The gentle sort of splendor
That surrounds the good and true.

A quiet, tender radiance
That filled the stable dim
And cast its benediction
On the faithful there with Him.

And may that gentle splendor
Shine for you through all the year
And halo all your hours
With hope and peace and cheer.

SISTERS

Now I can understand how Mary felt
On that first Christmas in the stable dim;
The sense of sweet fulfillment, joy and peace,
The humble pride that she had mothered Him.

Tonight there is no shining Eastern star;
No angel voices carol "Peace on earth,"
No Wise Men come to marvel from afar –
Yet I, too, know the miracle of birth.

And Mary, on her bed of straw, and I
Are sisters, sharing life's most wondrous joy –
We each have born a son of God and man –
We each have born a precious baby boy.

59

THAT NIGHT

The air was chill that night for Bethlehem,
But clear and bright – almost as light as day.
One star, I mind, hung nearly lantern-low
Above the place, as if to show the way.

The stable boy had come to fetch me there.
Some poor young mother's time had come, he said.
The inn was crowded, so the Child was born
With nothing but a manger for a bed.

I mind I took some blankets and some broth.
I pitied her – until I saw her face.
Such happiness was there, you'd not believe –
It glowed like candlelight in that dark place.

The Baby was a husky little Boy,
And beautiful – as all new babies are.
I fancied there was light around Him, too.
Though, doubtless, 'twas the glow from that low star.

You should have heard the way she crooned to Him.
He was her first, and her so young and fair.
They made a picture you'd not soon forget,
That little family in the stable there.

The father was a carpenter by trade.
I doubt his life had been an easy one.
He had a workman's hands, rough-worn and strong,
But gentle as a woman's with his Son.

I mind some shepherds came to see the Babe,
Big, burly fellows from the hills nearby.
They had a strange and babbling tale to tell
Of angels singing praises in the sky.

I mind the way she listened, how she smiled
Upon those strangers gazing at her Boy.
"I'm sure if we could hear," I mind she said,
"At every birth the angels sing for joy."

I've often wondered what became of them,
And what that little Fellow grew to be.
It seems it can't be thirty years have gone,
Yes, more than thirty, really – thirty-three.

CHRISTMAS PRAYER

Now, once more, guided by the Star,
The world has journeyed from afar
And, for awhile, has known surcease
From hate, before the Prince of Peace.

This Christmas night, Lord, we would pray –
Would thank Thee for this blessed day;
May something of its warmth and cheer
Stay with us all throughout the year.

The carols with their moving strain –
The poignant trips down memory's lane –
This day of merriment and mirth –
Help us to hold its deeper worth.

And, as the Wise Men Thou didst show
The surer, better way to go –
So may we, from this holy day,
Take up our lives a better way.

LIVING STORY

Make my heart a humble stable,
    Let the Christ Child cradle there.
Make my ears attuned to angels,
    Let my lips their tidings share.

Make my eyes reflect the glory
    Of the Star that led the way;
Make my life a living story
    Of that first glad Christmas Day.

ONLY FIVE MILES

Only five miles beyond Bethlehem,
    Jerusalem waits with its tree;
Only five miles from the manger birth
    To the grove of Gethsemane.

Only five miles from where the Star shone
    To mark where the Christ Child lay –
Only five miles to Golgotha's hill
    Up that cruel and bitter way.

Only five miles and thirty-three years
    In the life of one gentle Man,
Yet all of life's meaning, the depth of all love,
    Are compassed in that small span.

FAITH REBORN

CHRISTMAS – Each time I heard the word
 The embers of my grief were stirred
Till flames again arose and curled
 Around the ruins of my world.
How could I face this time of cheer
 Without that one I held so dear?

But one can never run away
 Or close the eyes to Christmas Day.
The spirit of it fills the air –
 It's here and there and everywhere.
I heard the songs, I saw the lights –
 The old familiar sounds and sights.

But it was not as it had been –
 I had no room in my heart's inn.
My mind, begrudging, gave Him space,
 But only in its stable place.
But that was all He asked of me –
 One thought where He might come to be.

One thought, so bleak, so manger-size –
 But when I lifted up my eyes,
The Star of Hope shone for me there,
 And angel voices filled the air.
I heard the bells on Christmas morn
 And knew the peace of faith reborn.

ONE SMALL CANDLE

As long as one small candle
Sends its beams into the night
To brighten dull, world-weary eyes
And guide them by its light;

As long as one small deed of love
Warms someone's lonely heart,
Or one word of forgiveness mends
Some friendship cleft apart;

As long as one hand lifts
A stumbling traveler on life's way,
Man has not quite forgotten
The Christ of Christmas Day.